Yes, you can enjoy using word processing software.   Dr. Canty Word Processing Workbook & Textbook

Yes, you can enjoy using word processing software, 1 byte at a time.
Yes, you can click with computers and the Internet, 1 byte at a time.
Yes, you can enjoy using word processing software, 1 byte at a time.

Name_____

CLASS EMAIL

ADDRESS_____

PASSWORD_____

Word Processing—Want or Need Computer Basic Skills?

New Creative Word Processing Workshop Projects & Activities
for Learning Most Versions of Microsoft Word

A DR. KATIE CANTY COMPUTER ACADEMY BASICS BOOK

Some Prior Internet & Typing Experience Helpful

Fun, easier, shorter, friendly learning activities

Yes, you can enjoy using word processing software, 1 byte at a time.
Yes, you can click with computers and the Internet, 1 byte at a time.
Yes, you can enjoy using word processing software, 1 byte at a time.

Dedication

To Jaimee who supports and attends
every technology academy event

To facility directors, class
participants, and alumni honor
graduates

Welcome

Go ahead now and hit the new, "Yes" Get Clicking with Computer Technology Button. Develop some basic word processing skills, or update your skills. Get the most out of what technology has to offer you.

Use your computer skills to prosper during every age. This basic word processing text workbook is the third book in the need or want technology skills book series.

Let's Get Started

You will engage in individual and/or team project activities to learn how to use technology and computers to enhance your life, and to share knowledge and wisdom.

Introduction

Users of our text work book bundles get active engagement and motivation from their classmates, Kenney and Barbara McCybers. The McCybers are the tech knowledge seeking couple introduced in Book 1, Seniors Need or Want Computer Skills? The couple is notorious for constantly asking anyone who comes around them for help with the computer and the other mobile device gifts that the children give them.

The McCybers will ask the young grand baby and even the smart Lassie puppy for tech "how to" help. With the completion of books in the bundle, the McCybers and their class mates keep becoming more and more tech savvy and a lot less tech knowledge dependent on family and strangers. The books in the bundle give participants like the McCybers the tech smarts start needed to complete their own tech tasks without pestering others for help all the time.

Mission/Vision Statement

The mission and vision of the computer technology academy via this word processing text workbook is technology life enrichment via the development of or updating of basic word processing skills by 100% of workshop completers.

Contents

Welcome Workshop Participant
Fill This in First

My full name is _____

Start date_____

Completion date_____

Name of professor & tutor_____

Senior center location _____

My email address is _____
My password_____
Each student has a new class email address. Check inside your course folder.

Your goal(s) _____

What do you plan to use your word processing skills for upon completion of this course?

_____

Your question(s)

Do you have a special question about computers, this class, or a suggestion? If so, write it here.

Welcome Workshop Participants

MISSION/VISION: COMPUTER TECHNOLOGY LITERACY, 1 BYTE AT A TIME

WORKSHOPS 1-12 SYLLABUS

WORKSHOP DATES: _____

TEXT: *Word Processing: Want or Need Computer Basic Skills?* by Dr. Katie Canty (available on amazon.com)

OUR PROFESSOR & TUTOR _____

GOAL: One hundred per cent of course completers should demonstrate an ability to digitally communicate using basic word processing skills.

INSTRUCTIONAL METHODS: Discussion, question & answer, online research, hands-on computer practice, student and team activities, individual or class project
Note: If needed or wanted, computer technology access and help are available in county libraries and community college libraries that have computers for public use.

COMMUNICATION: Preferred method of communication:

_____

CLASS PROCEDURES
- Cell phones on silence or vibrate before class begins
- Food/beverage consumption allowed in designated area(s)—not on or near computer work station
- Restroom facilities used on an as-needed basis

10 minutes
Review and/or completion of past week's workshop(s)
35 minutes
Introduction and discussion of current week's new material

10 minutes ------ BREAK TIME

35 minutes
Individual student lab work completion
10 minutes
Preview of upcoming week's topics and computer labs
5 minutes
Participant chat session: suggestions, clarifications, announcements

PERFORMANCE OBJECTIVES AND EXPECTATIONS

In addition to demonstration of attentiveness, thoughtfulness, and respect, there are four things that each participant is expected to demonstrate upon completion of 10 or more workshops:

1. create, save, edit, send, post, and/or print project and activity documents
2. use the Internet to get information from a website
3. complete the final (optional, depending upon participant)

WORKSHOPS CLASS HOURS
1.5　hours　per workshops
1.5　hours　practice

PREREQUISITES
- some prior computer keyboarding/typing experience very helpful
- USB Flash/Jump Drive (optional purchase)

ATTENDANCE
Attend scheduled workshop(s)--1 time a week for a little under 2 hours

GRADES
Upon completion of 8 or more workshops and the final exam, a workshop certificate document will be issued by the professor, preferably during the academy graduation celebration.

ACADEMY CELEBRATION CEREMONY – CERTIFICATE
For course completers in attendance at the senior technology academy celebration ceremony, an instructor's certificate of participation will be presented to each student during the ceremony. A prestigious, valedictorian-like MOUSE PAD HONOR AWARD will be presented to a selected student(s).

Ceremony participation is highly encouraged, however, participation is optional. Information will be given to students in time for invitations to be sent to family, friends, co-workers, club members, etc.

WORKSHOP 1

Treasure Hunt &
WORD Talk

What do I press, touch, mash, or swipe to get started?

"In all your getting, get understanding." Proverbs

WORKSHOP 1

- Understand the use of a few basic WORD terms.
- *Project 1*: Go on a Treasury Department treasure hunt mission.
- *Activity 1:* Open, prepare, and save a few sentences report document about the mission results.
- *Show & Tell Me How Presentations*
- *Self-Test*

*Note: Terms in bold like **software** and **URL box** are covered in Book 1 of the Senior Tech workshop book series.

Word Terminology Talk

Most computers today come with a word processing program which allows the user to write documents. The first step in learning how to use a **word processing software** program is to understand the terminology that is unique to word processing programs. Here are a few basic terms that will help.

ribbon	commands organized in tabs & menus that help you create a document **Where is the ribbon located?** Open the word processing program. Look to the top of the screen. You are looking at the ribbon when you see words that might include File, Home, Insert, Layout, etc.
spell/ grammar check	a squiggly red line under words that may be misspelled; a squiggly green line under words that may be grammatically incorrect
word processing	document preparation software for putting in information, formatting, editing, posting, and printing
word wrap	text goes to the next line automatically without having to press the enter key

Department of the Treasury
Treasure Hunt

Workshop 1   Project 1

step 1. Open the Internet.

step 2. Look to the top of the screen to find the white **URL box**. If there is any writing in it, press backspace or delete to clear out the letters.

step 3. Key in NC state treasury unclaimed property OR if from NC just follow this link: https://www.nctreasurer.com/Claim-Your-Cash/Claim-Your-NC_Cash/Pages/Search.aspx

step 4: Key in the LAST NAME 1st, press enter or click in the next box. Key in the first name last. Key in the blue search box and enter. Did you find your name? Enter the name(s) of family, too.

Find anything? Any state's unclaimed property website can be searched. Search for unclaimed property in states where you are relatives may have previously lived.

Your Treasure Hunt Report Document
Workshop 1   Activity 1

First, view the online how to presentations for Workshop 1. Next, prepare a 3 to 5 sentence, double space report about your treasure hunt experience. Save and print 1 hard copy.

step 1: Take a look at the two examples. In Workshop 1, write a report. The images will be added in Workshop 2. This is how to write the few sentences report.

step 2: With the computer on, open Word by selecting the icon with the white "W" on the blue background.

step 3: When Word opens, look to the top of the screen. Select File, New, Blank Document.

step 4: **Center align** the title, your name, and the workshop/class like in one of the examples.

To find center alignment, look to the top of the screen. Select the Home Tab on the Ribbon. Look down to the second row, near where the word paragraph appears. Select the second row of lines for center alignment.

step 5: To **boldface,** highlight the title and your name. If highlighted correctly, the words will appear shaded. Look to the top of the screen, and select the Home Tab, and the B for **bold**. Does the title and your name appear darker?

step 6: Key 3 or sentences about your results.

step 7: To **double space** the sentences, highlight the sentences. Right click the highlighted sentences. When the box opens, select Paragraph. Change before and after to zero. In the line spacing box, click the scroll symbol and select double.

step 8: **Save** the report to your own computer at home, look to the top of the Word screen. Click the save icon which is the picture of a disk. To save in class to your **USB**, look to the top of the Word screen, select the word File, Save As— not Save. Next, select Browse, USB drive. Type a new name for the document: Treasure Report Activity 1. Now, select the word "Save."

step 9: Print a **hard copy**. Be sure that the printer is turned on. To print, look to the top of the Word screen. Select File, Print. Place the hard copy print out in your class folder.

Treasure Hunt Results
$1,475.32 Richer Now
by Alan Wiley, Tech Workshop for Seniors

It is exciting to know that I am owed a piece of money instead of owing someone else money. The unclaimed funds are from an old house insurance policy. The extra money is going to my fishing trip fund. When I called, I found out that it might take up to 2 months in this state to get the check. I hope the fish are still running good when the check gets here.

Treasure Hunt Results Report
by Peg Tootle, Senior Center Tech Class

Yelp, I found that my husband's name shows up. I will tell him about this book and the class. My name did not come up. I am going to search for the names of my best friends and next door neighbors to see what turns up.

How-To Video Viewing Workshop 1

www.youtube.com

Conduct a YouTube word processing basics search. Select and watch a video of your choice that will show and tell you how to:

- create and save a new Word document
- open an existing Word document

www.gcflearnfree.org/

Get additional help producing your Word report document with these tutorials. When you open the site a dialogue box shows "What Can We Teach You." In this box, key in Word. Select and complete these short tutorials.

- Getting to Know Word
- Text Basics
- Formatting Text
- Page Layout

Important: There are different update versions of Word out there like Word 2010, Word 2013, Word 2016, and maybe future under construction versions. Skills are usually transferable between the different versions.
If possible, view presentations that are relevant to the Word version on your device/computer.

your treasure hunt report

Workshop 1 Self-Test

Circle the alphabet that shows the correct response to each statement.

1. **Microsoft Office Word is**:
A.   a word processing software program
B.   a program for spread sheet preparation
C.   the most popular hardware program
D.   none of the above

2. **To use word processing software**:
A.   the Internet must be up and running
B.   the printer must be turned on
C.   a USB drive has to be available
D.   the program has to be on the device

3. **To open a document previously saved in Word, go to**:
A.   File, New
B.   Home, View
C.   File, Open
D.   Review, Document

4. **To _remove_ boldface from a word**:
A.   Select the word, and press the backspace key.
B.   Go to the Home tab, and select delete until the bold disappears.
C.   Select the word first, then press the shaded B on the Home tab.
D.   none of the above

WORKSHOP 2

Illustrate
with Pictures
1,2, 3 Draw

Word Art and Images: How do I put in these pictures?

"A picture is worth a thousand words."
Banard

WORKSHOP 2

- Understand the use of a few basic WORD terms.

- *Project 2:* Explore some currently cool and useful public domain images websites.

- *Activity 2:* Cut and paste art images to the report document prepared in Activity 1.

- *Activity 3:* Make your name a work of art with Word Art features.

Word Terminology Talk 2

Let's talk about terms that you may encounter as you learn to use word processing commands to add images to a document. Adding just the right image(s) to a document can be like adding stars to a romantic night time sky or sun rays to a cloudless sky during vacation days.

cut	remove selected words, cells, or objects from a document; represented by a scissors icon
paste	add previously cut or copied words, cells, or objects to a document
Word Art	changing the look of a word(s) by specifying such things as the font, shape, size, color, texture, outline, and special effects
Home	a tab on the Ribbon to select in order to change or create new document settings like line spacing, font type, or adding bullets, etc.
fonts	various designs, sizes and shapes of alphabets, numbers, and symbols

Art Image(s) for Your Report
Workshop 2   Project 1

These are two among many public domain sites with thousands of free photos and clipart images. Select a money art image from one of the sites listed here. Open the report document from Workshop 1. Copy and paste a money image(s) in your treasure hunt report.

- http://publicdomainvectors.org/

- https://pixabay.com/

How to Go to an Internet Website

step 1: With the Internet up, use the delete key or backspace key to get rid of any writing that might already be in the URL box. Key in a new website address: your choice--public domain website or pixabay. Press the enter key after accurately typing the web address of your choice.

step 2: When the website opens, find the site's search box. Type in the word money. Which money image do you like best? The money image you like best will be added to you treasure hunt report.

Copying or Cutting Then Pasting Images
Workshop 2   Activity 1

When an image is cut, the image is removed and the image is no longer where it was--like cutting something away with scissors. When an image is copied, the original image stays where it is, but a replica—a copy of the image is made to be placed in a different document.

Copy and paste the money image of your choice into your treasure hunt report document.

How to Open Word
step 1: Open Word. To do this select the icon on the start menu with the big "W" or the name Word.
How to Open the Report Saved to Your USB

step 2: Open your treasure hunt report document. To do this, insert your USB drive into a removable drive port on your device/computer. Look to the top of the screen to the Ribbon. Select File, Open. Click on removable drive and the name of your treasure hunt report document to open it.

How to Copy and Paste

step 3: Go back to the money image of your choice, and click on it. A hand will appear and a dialogue box. Click Copy image.

step 4: Go to the end of your treasure hunt report. Right click and a dialogue box appears. Click Paste. Click the pasted picture and use the star and circles to adjust the placement of the money image so that it looks good.

My Word Art Master Piece Creation
Workshop 2   Activity 2

Word Art draws attention to text by adding definition and making text standout. Make your name a work of art. See the singer and super hero examples.

step 1: Open Word. Look to the top of the Word screen. Click the Insert tab on the ribbon. Look for the word art button. There will be a slanted A on the word art button. Select one of the styles shown. A rectangular text box will open. Delete the text from the box.

step 2: Key your first and last name in the box, or just for fun, give yourself a title as shown in the examples. Click the box until a 6-prone star and smaller white circles appear. Click on the star and drag your name box nearer to the center of the page. Click and drag the smaller circles to make your name smaller or larger.

step 3: Click your name until the box reappears. Look to the top of the screen and find Format, Drawing Tools. Enhance your name box by adding a Texture fill, Shape outline, Text Effect/Transform, or 3D rotation. Click on Theme styles and add color. Which Transform and 3D rotation effect do you like best?

step 4: Take a **selfie** or use a public domain royalty free image. A selfie is a picture that you take of yourself. Position the camera device so that you are in the shot. Save the selfie or the image to your USB drive as selfieactivity3. Insert the selfie picture under your word art name.

step 5: Save your name word art to your USB. Print 1 hard copy, and place it in your class folder.

Avon Walker, Singer
Newport Voices of Praise

your word art masterpiece

Formatting Practice Homework
Workshop 2   Activity 3

The **Home tab** on the **Ribbon** is used to format text so that a document will look professional and/or appealing. With Word open, look to the top of the screen on the Ribbon to find the Home tab.

Bold, Underline, Italics
step 1: **Practice bolding, underlining, and italicizing** your name. With Word open, select the home tab on the Ribbon and click the B. Start keying your name. This will bold everything as it is typed. Be sure to click the B again to stop bolding. The bold, italicize, and underline keys are toggles. A toggle key turns a command on and turns it off again like a light switch on the wall. To underline, highlight your name by clicking in front of it, then moving the mouse over it. The color will change which is highlighting. Look to the top of the screen. Click or press the I to italicize, and the U to underline. Click again to turn off italicize and underline.

Undo and Redo
step 2: The Undo and Redo buttons are like your best friends when using word processing software. Look to the top of the screen, and located the two curved arrows on the Ribbon. These are the Undo and Redo buttons. Click the first curved arrow to undo removing the BIU features.

Font Type, Size, Color

step 3: Add Arial, size 16, red color to your name by highlighting your name. Right click the highlighted name. When the dialogue box appears, select Font and the color red from the listed theme colors. Does each letter of your name appear in red?

Margin Setting

step 4: Set a new Wide margin setting of 2 inches on the left and the right. Margins are already preset for Normal margins of 1 inch on the right and left of a screen page. If you need to change margin settings, select the **Layout tab** on the Ribbon. Look to the top of the screen to find the Ribbon with the Home tab on it. Click Layout, Margins, Wide. If you want to specify other margin sizes, not listed, click on the Custom button and key in the margin size numbers that you need.

Bulleted Lists

step 5: Make a bulleted list of any one of the following:
- the 3 TV game shows that I like best of all
- my personal list of 3 favorite spots team players
- the top 3 best movies that I have ever seen

To make the bulleted list, select the Home tab and look for the icon with the dotted periods and lines. Select it. Did a dot appear? Begin keying your list. Press enter to make the next bullet dot.

Printing

step 6: Save then print 1 hard copy of your homework document and place it in your folder.

your document: name bold, underline, and in red, size 16 font Arial; margins 1.5 inches on both sides; your bulleted list

Very Important: Saving--Save and Save As

Time spent formatting and preparing a document can easily be wasted unless your word processing document is saved in a timely manner in a location where you can find it again. If you save your document on a public computer or a classroom device, it usually will be deleted and cannot be retrieved again later.

Save As - If you are saving a document for the *first time*, look to the top of the screen on the Ribbon. Select File, Save As and specify where you want to save your document— removable device like your USB, or to **the cloud**, or another network place.

Save – Click on the disk icon picture to save a document right back again to the same location where you previously saved it in Save As. Be sure to save your document(s) before leaving a work session. It you do not save a document; it is like it was never done or you do not need it again. It is a very good idea to click the Save icon picture on the Ribbon before during and after a document preparation session.

Online Presentation Viewing Activities
Workshop 2

www.youtube.com

View two, short how to presentations. Go to YouTube.
Enter a search for:

- How to save a Word document to a flash drive & open it
- How to cut and paste a picture in Word

www.gcflearnfree.org/
Complete the Creating Word Art Tutorial.

Note: A flash drive is also known as a USB or a thumb drive.

Workshop 2   Self-Test

Correctly specify which statement is true or false by writing the word **True** _or_ **False** by each statement.

_____1. In order to paste, something must first be selected, cut or copied before it can be pasted.

_____2. Word is the most popular hard ware in use today.

_____3. There are several tabs on the Ribbon to help with writing, editing, and printing a document(s).

_____4. The Insert tab on the Ribbon, will allow you to save a picture to your USB.

WORKSHOP 3

Get an Update on Best Practices: Using Word for Social Networking

Our association posts upcoming events and other great stuff on social media, how do I see the association posts and maybe respond?

"When you give everyone a voice and give people power, the system usually ends up in a pretty good place." Mark Zuckerberg

Post, Pin, Tag, or Tweet
Workshop 3   Project 1

Networking is using social media to reach out and touch others via the exchange of information. One of the best things about social media sites like **Facebook** is that you can see the past, present, and upcoming events **postings** of friends, family, or businesses. You can play games that let you help each other out--games like Candy Crush or Sudoku. You can make new friends, search for old friends from high school, old jobs, or just find someone you lost contact with and want to see what they are up to.

Update 1: Relationships and social networks are of upmost importance. Social network sites like Facebook, Twitter, Instagram, Twitter, Pinterest, Periscope, Youtube, etc. are really big business. Friends and family everywhere post, pin, tag, and tweet--sometimes too much but networking is still a great way to keep in touch.

Update 2: Businesses without social media presence, may not be businesses at all for any significant length of time. Most people are expected to have some kind of social network presence or activity that can be viewed by others. Do you have presence—social media presence, yet?

Already on Facebook, complete steps 4 and 5. If you just want to see how to network, go to the beyond computer basics or Chapel Bowen Face book page. The professor　　　will log you in so that you can network from one of these participant page(s), or the professor may select another Facebook page for you to post and network from.

Do you want your own Facebook place? Complete steps 1-5.
step 1: Go to facebook.com
step 2: Select Sign Up.
step 3: Key the requested information in the fill in sign up boxes. Your email address and password will be needed. Fill in your **Profile** information.

Friend Me
Workshop 3　Activity 1

Make a new friend(s) on Facebook.
step 1. Click in the URL box.
step 2. Type in facebook.com.
step 3. Log into your Facebook account or post from a Facebook page specified by the professor.
step 4. In the Search Facebook dialogue box that will appear at the top of the screen, key in beyond computer basics. Send a friend request to beyond computer basics. Key in the name of a relative, neighbor, or associate. If their name shows up on Facebook, you decide whether you want to send them a friend request.

Social Network
Workshop 3　　Activity 2

step 1. Prepare a new message post about your participation in our senior life technology workshop(s).

step 2. Add a new photo or use a picture from your USB or an image from a royalty free Internet site like Pixabay. Select the image of a digital camera when you are ready to add your Facebook photo.

step 3. Click Post when you finish preparing the message and image. If you need to change/edit anything select the inverted v icon. Make desired changes then click post.

About Using Word Processing for Social Networking

Are you considering posting a weekly or daily message like an inspirational short story or lengthy wisdom quote of the day? If so, it is often easier to prepare the post message in Word first, then cut and paste it into your social media post.

WORKSHOP 4

Make Your Own Fee-Free Greeting Cards

A Card: How Do I Make It Say & Look Like I Want?

"Creativity is contagious, pass it on."
Albert Einstein

WORKSHOP 4

- *Project 3*: Go to a free online digital card making website. Select, personalize, and email a card of your choice to Dr. Canty at techseekers@yahoo.com.

- *Activity 4*: Use a Word template to construct, and personalize a greeting card. Print the card and give it to someone that you know will appreciate it.

Card Making
Workshop 4   Project 1

An eCard is a digital, rather than a printed hard copy, greeting card that is usually sent via email. 123 Greetings is a free online card making website that allows users to select and send a greeting card for most popular occasions. The digital cards play songs like Happy Birthday, make noise, familiar sounds, and show moving images.

eCard—Make and Send Your Own Card(s) Online

Which eCard at 123 Greetings is going to be your favorite?

step 1: Go to http://www.123greetings.com/

step 2: Take a few minutes to browse through the different card themes. Then, select a card of your choice.

step 3: Customize the card by adding a personal message.

step 4: Send the eCard to someone whose email address you know, and who will likely appreciate your sending a card. If you prefer, send your eCard to Professor Canty at techseekers@@yahoo.com. Be sure not to key the last period of the email address. The last period is punctuation and not part of the email address.

Template Card: Make & Print Yours
Workshop 4   Activity 1

A word processing template has pre-set formatting designs for you to add your words and/or pictures.

step 1: **Open templates**--Go to the Ribbon, File, New.

step 2: **Key in what you are looking for**--In the search for templates dialogue box, key in the words holiday cards. If you prefer, select another card type like birthday card.

step 3. **Select --** Look at some of the templates and select a template card of your choice by clicking on it.

step 4: **Customize** by keying your name in the From section. If you want to change the message already there to a personal message, delete out the pre-printed words. Key in your own choice of words. See the template example.

step 5 (optional): **Customize by inserting a picture(s)**. Do you have a picture(s) saved to **the cloud** or on your USB that would make your card look more appealing? The selfie from workshop 2 could be inserted. Click the template picture to see if a dialogue box opens that says Change Picture. To insert your own picture, look to the top of the screen and find the **Insert tab** on the Ribbon. Select Pictures. Specify the location, like removable drive for the USB, of the picture in order to select and insert it.

step 6: **Save** the template as mycardworkshop3.

step 7: **Print** 2 copies. A copy to give and another to place in your workshop folder.

Yes, a few card templates may look upside down until printed and folded.

Example: sides 1 and 2 of a Word card template

...see   the

reason for Christmas on
my handmade Bible quilt

**Card made for you
in Columbus Center
word processing workshop**

by Mrs. Lillie Young

**Christmas
gift ideas - suggestions**

To your enemy, forgiveness.
To an opponent, tolerance.
To a friend, your heart.
To God, love.
To all, charity.
To every child, a good example.
To yourself and others, respect.

Created just
for you son

by your
Grand Dad

Happy Birthday

Hope your birthday
is a slice of
cake!

May a wish come
true for each layer.

from Rev. Levi Hester, Sr.
creative word processing
Continuing Education Dept.

your greeting card

Workshop 4   Self-Test

Terminology Talk 3 Online Research: Conduct Internet research to help you respond. Write an appropriate response.

1. template: What is the purpose of a word processing template?
2. the cloud: Where is it?
3. app: An app: what is one that you use or would like to use?
4. website: A fun, humorous, or informative website that you like—list the URL here.

WORKSHOP 5

Brain Train with Word Processing Neurobics

**Aerobics for Your Senses
Everlasting brain power—fact
or science fiction?**

"Man is still the most extraordinary computer of all."   John F. Kennedy

WORKSHOP 5

- **Project 1**: Take an online neurobics quiz like the quiz at http://www.keepyourbrainalive.com/quiz

- **Activities 1-3**: Complete the senses word processing neurobics activities.

touching and seeing
Workshop 5 Activity 1

How fast can you make these words shape like a tree?

**Of
all the
saws I ever
saw saw I never
saw a saw that could
saw as this saw saws!
Peter Piper picked a peck of
pickled peppers. If Peter Piper picked
a peck of pickled peppers, how many pickled
peppers did Peter Piper pick?
Centering
this
poem
is
very
fun!!**

step 1: Key the words exactly as shown. Key Of, press the enter key; Type all the, press enter, and so on.

step 2: Finish keying the poem and select it. If selected, the shading should appear darker.

step 3: Look to the top of the screen on the Ribbon. Locate the Home tab and click on the center alignment icon. Is your poem now in the shape of a tree?

step 4: Save your document as poemtreeworkshop4. Print and place a hard copy in your folder.

your tree shaped poem

hearing

Workshop 5   Activity 2

Try getting a message across to someone using a new method of communication in which only the title of 3 or less songs can be stated to communicate. Yeah, the songs can be sung, but this is not required—if you prefer, just state the song(s) title.

- I Can Fly (song)
- It's A Small World (song)

What is the message?

_____

seeing, tasting, hearing, feeling

Workshop 5   Activity 3

Let someone know where you would like to travel by stating just 4 main clues about the location that only tell what the location is known for as far as taste, sight, sound, and feel.

- sight clue--gondolas
- taste clue—pizza
- sound clue---bells
- feel clue—rocking back and forth

What is the location? _____

Workshop 5   Self-Test

Create your own new neurobics exercise activity. This can be done as an individual or as a team/group.

step 1: Give your new neurobics exercise a name/title. Key, center, and bold the title.

step 2: Include your name and the name of any team member(s).

step 3: Describe what the objective of your neurobics exercise is. Key the details.

step 4: Save as neurobicsworkshop. Post your neurobics workshop responses and self-test to our social network site or send an email message with your neurobics completed document attached. The email address is: beyondcomputerbasics@yahoo.com.

step 5: (optional) Print 1 hard copy and place it in your class folder.

your own new neurobics exercise activity

WORKSHOP 6

Get an Update on Best Practices: Using Word Processing for Blogging & Online Selling

Will people actually pay good money for this old thing?

"If you have just one reader and your blog changes their life, your blog is big enough."
Darren Rouse

WORKSHOP 6

Project 1: Select an item to sell online—just for practice. Obtain pricing information pertaining to the item from an online selling site.

Activities 2: Take and save photos of the selected item.

Activities 3: Make a descriptive bullet list in Word about the item that you selected. Note the best practices included in some of the steps.

Project 2:   Write a blog entry.

One Man's Trash Is Another Man's Treasure
Turning Trash into Treasure Online

Do you make crafts, have stuff from the old days, or have unused closet purchases that you want to get rid? Vast numbers of consumers frequent sites like Amazon and eBay in a single day--an estimated 70 to 100 million.

People who make crafts really like etsy.com. People who write books, or want to sell books like amazon.com. The largest online market places in the world are Amazon & eBay.

Best Practices

VERY, VERY IMPORTANT: When opening a new online selling account for a site like eBay, write down your user name and password, immediately, as soon as it is entered and accepted. Email user names and passwords to yourself. If using eBay, write down access codes for both accounts--the eBay account and for PayPal account. If you do not enter the right user name and password, the accounts will not open.

1. If an item is difficult to package and mail, avoid listing it.

2. If you do not know the value, do not list an item until a thorough research of the price is conducted. The value may be hidden in the fact that some items like old high school class rings and really old computers may contain gold.

3. Be prepared to monitor an item several times before, during, and after the sale.

4. Ship right away—like within a day or two of getting paid. As soon as an item gets a bid, this may be a good time to get it ready for shipping.

5. Save the tracking numbers printed on the mailing receipt. After mailing, a good practice is to provide the bidder with the shipping tracking number. There is usually a place to do this in the sold column.

6. Watch out for messy bidders who may ask a lot of questions but do not bid. Watch out for customers who want price adjustments before or after bidding.

Workshop 6 Activity 1

step 1: Select a product to sell online. What product did you select?

step 2: Go to ebay.com. Key in the name of the item to see if there are similar items like your item already listed? This will clue you in as to how to best list your item and for what price.

Workshop 6 Activity 2

step 1: Take at least 12 pictures of the item from all sides.

step 2: Take a close up on any signatures, labels, inscriptions, markings, or defects. If the item is clothing include measurements. If the item is a book, include a picture of the print history line and ISBN number.

Workshop 6 Activity 3

Key a listing description of the item in Word. A good title is essential and should capture a potential buyer's attention. Describe the item with a short-bulleted list and include condition as one of the bulleted items.

Condition is important. If there is anything less than perfect about an item that is not new, be sure to include the details-- like from a smoke-free, pet free home, or shows scratches and smudges, or missing a something. See the examples.

rare Star Wars The Darth Jar Jar Toy from 2002, UNUSED in original package

- could prove the theory that Jar Jar Binks is a Sith Lord
- released one time in 2002
- figures measures 3 inches tall
- more information at darthjarjartoy.com
- **condition**: tattered original package with smudges, and scratches, and cardboard edge peel as shown in the photos; been packed away in storage for a while

**FILSON HUNT JACKET OUTDOOR COAT
Size M Green 100% Cotton Seattle**

- right to left across the back= 18 inches
- sleeve length= 24 inches long
- jacket length from edge of back collar to bottom= 24 inches
- size M shown on the label
- **condition**: name written in black marker and 3 numbers written on the inside label, overall good clean condition

**Vintage Lot 7 Dr. Seuss hard copy books
stated 1st editions +1 old Paperback**

- books 2-7 are hard backs
- purchased at different times of release a long time ago
- 4 of the hard covers state 1st edition
- book 1--the paperback in acceptable condition and shows a tattered cover and beigey pages
- **condition**: ranges from good to fair minus; orange book has dust jacket tare as shown in the photos; 1 book has lots dust spot edges; inside page edge creases in 1; dust jacket scratches and smudges

Workshop 6   Project 2

Key your blog using a Word blog template. Go back later and publish or comment on our class blog at:
https://seniorlife.tech.blog/
Blogs focus on a particular topic and most have a method to allow visitors to leave comments.
Many blogs focus on a particular topic such as health, sports, web design, or mobile technology. Other blogs are like personal journals that present the author's daily life and thoughts.

Some are more eclectic with creative blog content like topics in the Under-Construction Blog List. Which of the blogs from the list would you be interested in reading? What is going to be the title and content of your new blog?

step 1: Select File, New. Wait for the white dialog box to open and key in the word blog. When the blog post template shows, click on it to select it. Create, Register Later. Select Create and a blog template will show.
step 2: Follow the prompts on the blog template. Enter the blog subject and blog content.
step 3: Save your blog. Print 1 hard cover and place it in your class folder.

New Under Construction Creative Blog Titles

Food
- Man who never eats
- $40 cronut doughnuts—Get em' while they'ar hot
- Panthers official football team chocolate chip cookie

Personal Life Experiences
Second hand Large Mart store infested with Alien
troll shoppers and workers—32-year diary of images

Travel
- Gold Mining Adventure Camp & No Way in…..Land
- Cape Fear Sea Walking & Moby Dick Cat Fishing

Professional & How to Advice
- Rich Mom, Poor Mom and Job, the Wisest Dad Guy
- Extract gold from real old computers

Product reviews
- Best Food for Your Alligator Turtle Friends
- No-cavities for life tooth polish
- Coloring Book of 30 Mancave designer toilets

Money making
Invest some sense, become a Millionaire in 60 Days

Fashion
New Invisible Blue Jeans

Fitness
Age 78 female body builder & age 100 track star

your online sales
listing description—hard copy

your blog message

Workshop 6　Self-Test
Complete either Step 1 OR Step 2.

step 1: Open your online sales description. Select a photo from the 12 photos taken in Activity 2 and add it to the description: This will be the main photo. The main photo is the photo that shows up first on an item's listing page. Save and print 1 hard copy of the description with the added main photo. Place it in your class folder.

step 2: Open your blog post. Add a photo to your blog post message. Find a royalty free image on the Internet or select a photo from your USB files. Save and print 1 hard copy or post your blog message in comments at: https://seniorlife.tech.blog/.

WORKSHOP 7

Play Ball 114

How can I play ball with up to 114 of my own words?

"Just play. Have fun. Enjoy the game."
Michael Jordan

WORKSHOP 7

- **Project 1**: Use the word count feature to help prepare a mini-short story of 114 words or less. See the examples.

- **Activity 1**: Use the insert pictures feature to help illustrate your true play ball story.

Play Ball 114 Document Formatting
Workshop 7   Project 1

Write a true 114 words of less mini-short story about something related to playing ball. The true story can be about any kind of ball—soccer, baseball, basketball, football, kick ball, t-ball, or a new kind of team sports ball playing, etc.

step 1: See the two examples.

step 2: Open Word. Set the right (inside) and left (outside) margins to 1.5 inches. Look to the top of the page on the Ribbon. Select the Layout Tab, Margins, Custom Margins. Scroll to 1.5 or key in 1.5 for both margins. Set line spacing for 1.5 by selecting Paragraph, Line Spacing, and keying or scrolling to 1.5.

step 3: Key and center a title for your story. Press Enter and key and center your name and the workshop name.

step 4: Key your true story. Keep up with the number of words by using the word count feature. The word count feature appears at the bottom of the screen in the newest version of Word. In past versions look to the Ribbon and select the Tools button, Word Count. How is it working out? Are you able to tell your true story with 114 words or less?

Play Ball 114 Inserting Pictures
Workshop 7   Activity 1

step 1: Insert a picture or two that illustrates your story. With the Internet up, key in search words like baseball clip art images. The examples contain royalty free clip art images.

step 2: Select and save the image(s) that best illustrates your story. Click on the image to select it. After selecting, right click and the Save As dialogue box will appear. Name and Save the image(s) to your USB or other findable location.

step 3: With your play ball document open, move the cursor to the place in the document where you want the image to appear. Look to the Ribbon and select Insert, Picture, then the Removeable Drive USB—or what location you saved the image to.

step 4: Select the picture and a 4-prone asterisk star like icon will appear with several white circles or white squares around it. Practice using drag and drop with the asterisk star icon to adjust the image size and position. Make the image larger or smaller by using the sizing handles which are the circles or squares. Resizing and repositioning images takes practice.

step 5: Save your document. Print 1 hard copy for your class folder and email attach a copy of your story to Dr. Canty at beyondcomputerbasics@yahoo.com.

I Fell In Love With Baseball
by Tim Long
Word Processing Workshop

I fell in love with baseball as a kid. My father did not want me to play. He wanted me to work on the farm. I had just finished the 8th grade. My best friend asked me to play in the Babe Ruth League that summer. I knew my father would say no, so I asked my mother. She said go ahead and play. We will deal with your Father later. My coach was my father's boss. He asked my father was I his son. The coach said that I was the best team player. My father started going to the games.

WE WON!
LITTLE LEAGUE BASEBALL WORLD SERIES
by Willie Robinson　　　　　　Activity 1 WS7

Back in 1998, I began to take my great-great grandson to play ball. As his team became older, progressed, and advanced in the sport, we became more and more active. They played all around at all the schools. It was a lot of fun at first, then it began to get very hard to keep up with traveling but then we got help. As time went on we won the state championship and went on to play in the world series, which was played in Beaufort, SC. We went on to win the **World Series little league**.

your play ball
114 words or less mini-story

Workshop 7   Self-Test

Message Preparation   Play Ball 114

A ball player like Hank Aaron of the Atlanta Braves or Michael Jordan, whose cousin LaDreama was a student in my class, is going to be asked to pick the best student write up about a real-life experience involving any kind of ball playing—racquet ball, nerf ball, tennis, golf, soccer, football, basketball, baseball, etc. The only catch is that the write-up can only have up to 114 or less words.

step 1: Conduct online research to find contact information for a popular local or national sports figure. Whose contact information did you find?

step 2: Prepare and send a message asking a sports star to pick the winner of our play ball 114 competition.

step 3: Send a copy of the message that you prepare to Dr. Canty at: beyondcomputerbasics@yahoo.com.

WORKSHOP 8

Create Your New Robot Species Flyer or Event Flyer

How Do I Get Started?

"Logic will get you from A to B, but imagination takes you everywhere."
Albert Einstein

WORKSHOP 8

- ***Project 1***: Use a Word template to construct a flyer about a new species of robot(s)—use your imagination. Be creative! <u>OR</u> If you prefer create a flyer that you can actually use for an upcoming event. See the examples.

Workshop 8   Project 1

step 1: With Word open, look to the top of the screen on the Ribbon. Select File, New. A white dialogue box will appear. Type in the word flyers. Hundreds of different flyer templates will appear.

step 2: Plan your flyer. Look through some of the flyers and select a flyer like the seasonal event flyer used to prepare the robot flyer in the example. Which of the template flyers is closest to what you want your flyer to look like? Select a flyer of your choice.

step 3: Save the selected flyer to your USB. Open the flyer from your USB. When you click on the picture does a dialogue box show up that reads, change picture? If not, go back and select a new flyer template which will allow for picture change.

step 4: Are you going to create a robot new species flyer or an event flyer? Search the Internet for a royalty free image(s) for the flyer or take new pictures with your cell or digital camera. Use the Save As command to save your selected picture image(s) to your USB.

step 5: Open the flyer template that you selected. Follow the template instructions like this: To replace any tip text with your own words, just click it and start typing. To replace the photo or logo with your own pictures, right-click it and then click Change Picture. To try our different looks for this flyer, on the Design Tab, check out the Themes, Colors, and Fonts galleries if you would like. Be patient, it may take more than a few tries to get the flyer like you want.

step 6: Save your new flyer. Print 1 hard copy and place it in your class folder.

CHEF MAC COOKS 4 U

certified robotic chef of the Whales Culinary Institute

serving in the finest homes and restaurants for over 10 years with an accident free 10-year record

several award-winning meal programs including the Barbie and Ken

- **Mac will scan your vitals and prepare food according to your nutritional need.**

- **Mac, the regional medical center robot chef(s): Rent by the week, month, or year. HURRY, Macs are going fast—only 17 left!**

pictured: meatless, gluten free 150 calorie barbecue burger with egg whites that look like a toasted bun

by Barbie McCybers, Vocational 2nd Career Program   ipwatchdog.com (image)

CHICKEN DINNERS

Friday, Dec. 17 & Saturday, Dec. 18 starts 11 AM

5929 Carolina Beach Road, Wilmington, NC 28401
Call for delivery of 4 or more dinners/sandwiches: 910-**762-5289**

Proceeds benefit BOWENS CHAPEL AME ZION SUNDAY SCHOOL

Chicken Dinners $7
Choice of Sides
Collards, Macaroni,
Potato Salad
Chicken Sandwiches $3.50

Barbecue Sandwiches with slaw $3.50

by Deloris Williams, Continuing Educ. Creative Word Processing Class

You're invited to the 10th annual

word processing robot
convention

Where: County Senior Center, 701 Robot Avenue, Silicon Valley, CA 90201
When: **February 29 of each leap year starting in 2020**
Time: 9 AM – 4 PM
Admission: Free

by Chris Hester   WP8   St. Luke's Tech Update Workshop
https://br.fotolia.com (image)

your new flyer

WORKSHOP 9

Tell Your
1-Sentence Tale
Fairy Tale Romance
with a Remarkable
Twist

What! What is a 1-sentence mini-short story tale?

"The way to get started is to quit talking and begin." Walt Disney

WORKSHOP 9

Project 1: What is the best short story remake or twist on a fairy tale that you can write in just 1 sentence? Go online to find out what 1-sentence short-stories look like.

Project 2: See the book of myths and folklore tales by fellow workshop participants. Go to amazon.com. Search for computer academy first book of short stories.

Activity 1: Create your own 1-sentence mini-short story. See the examples.

Activity 2: Become a published author!

The 12 Dancing Princes

And the winning prince dancers are: Elvis gyrating his hips; Blackbeard shivering his limb timbers; Jackson moon walking his legs; and Travolta brow sweating out his Saturday night fever.

by Ed Robert Carter (alias Blackbeard)
creative word processing, continuing education

Mr. Romeo and Mrs. Juliet

Romeo and Juliet eloped, escaped, and existed happily ever after in a place like Canada, but it was their "get along on an as needed basis families" who concocted that story about the couple committing suicide to save face and to prevent members of their aristocracy from marrying anyone a Big Daddy deemed "unfit."

by Isaac Montague McDougal, VIII   WP Workshop 8

The Beauty & The Beast Ball

Meet Muffet a 34-year-old medical doctor desperately seeking a cure for cancer, and meet 29-year old Aladdin the surfer dude and heir to the Iron Chef Throne still searching for his soul mate: So, what happens when the two meet, trash the curds and whey, and go out for coffee after the Beauty and the Beast Ball?

by Madison Green   Word Processing Workshop 8

Workshop 9   Project 1

step 1: Online research to find out what 1-sentence short-stories look like. Does any of these 1-sentence stories provide inspiration for you to write your story?

step 2: Online research the topic, top ten fairy tales. Which fairy tale are you going to remake with a twist? Yes, you can create your own new fairy tale.

Workshop 9   Project 2

Go to amazon.com. Search for computer academy first book of short stories. Which of the titles appeals to you most?

Workshop 9   Activity 1

step 1: Read the 1-sentence fairy tale remake with a twist examples.

step 2: Decide on a fairy tale that you will remake. Open Word and key your 1-sentence story.

step 3: Set 1.5 inch left and right margins. Set line spacing for double. Key the title in bold. Add your name and the name of the workshop below your sentence.

step 4: Save and print a hard copy. Place the hard copy in your class folder.

Workshop 9   Activity 2

If you would like to see your 1-sentence mini short story published in the academy's first book of 1-sentence short stories, email attach a copy to beyondcomputerbasics@yahoo.com. Be sure to include the name that you want to use to credit you for your mini-story contribution.

your 1-sentence mini fairy tale

WORKSHOP 10

Edible Word Processing Project: Make a Candy Scroll for Imparting Wisdom

Will friends like my edible word processing project?

"Friends are smarties in the candy bowl of life."
Smarties Candy Co.

WORKSHOP 10

- Project 1: Use the table draw feature.

- Activity 1: Convert words into a table.

make an edible word processing craft
Workshop 10   Project 1

step 1: Check out "candy gift scroll messages images" on Pinterest. Do any of the candy gift scrolls appeal to you?

step 2: Decide on a theme for your scroll. Come up with 5 sayings or messages related to your theme.

step 3: Things to Assemble

- Five different pieces of small candies related to the message or theme of your choice
- scotch tape
- scissors
- gift ribbon
- decorative bag to place the scroll in
- white or light colored paper like construction printing paper

step 4: Open Word. Look to the top of the screen to the Ribbon. Select Insert, Table, Draw Table. Do you see a transparent image of a pen/pencil?

step 5: Move the pencil from left to right and draw a box shape. With the pencil make 20 horizontal lines.

step 6: Key a title based on your theme--in all caps, bold, centered, on the first row. On the second line, key a subtitle. On the 3rd line key your first message. Skip 2-3 horizontal lines and add your next message. Continue keying each of the 5 sayings or messages, leaving space to tape a small candy between messages. See the Wisdom Candy Scroll example.

step 7: Key your name, the location, and title of the workshop. Save your document as candyscrollwp11.

step 8: Place the thicker construction paper like sheet in the printer. Print a hard copy.

step 9: Either to the right of the message or under the message, tape a candy appropriate to the saying or message. Gently roll the paper up to shape like a scroll. Add a really small piece of tape to the middle to secure it. Tie a decorative ribbon neatly around the center and place it in a bag as shown in the example.

step 10: Give your candy gift scroll to someone who you know will appreciate it.

WISDOM CANDY SCROLL

This holiday season, remember …

Jesus is peace during life's crackles and pops. (miniature Hersey crackle candy bar)

Chew on the Word of **God** daily. (stick of gum)

Jesus is the only thing that really satisfies. (Hersey Kiss)

Break out into **happiness** because he lives. (miniature almond joy candy bar)

The **joy** of the season is minty cool and refreshing. (mint in a wrapper)

From _____

Your Sunday School Teacher

Leland Center Word Processing   Workshop 11 Project 1

Each scroll has 5 sayings or words of advice
with a candy reflecting each saying: Example,
a small single-size cellophane wrapped Life
Saver candy with the message...if you need a
Life Saver you can count on me!

scrolls by Novella Hasty, Leland Senior Center
Creative Word Processing Workshop 10

your wisdom scroll document picture or print out

convert text to a table
Workshop 10 Activity 1

step 1: Open Word. Key a list of the names of the 5 different candies used to make your candy scroll—a list like this with each candy listed on a separate line.

Hersey snap, crackle, pop miniature bar
stick of gum
miniature Almond Joy
single Hersey Kiss in silver foil
mint in a wrapper

step 2: Highlight the list of candies. Look to the top of the screen on the Ribbon. Select Insert, Table, Convert text to table.

Hersey snap, crackle, pop miniature bar
stick of gum
miniature Almond Joy
single Hersey Kiss in silver foil
mint in a wrapper

WORKSHOP 11

Prepare Your Better Than Theirs Resume & Cover Letter

What Kind of Resume and Letter Gets Most Job Seekers Hired?

"Pleasure in the job puts perfection in the work." Aristotle

WORKSHOP 11

- **Project 1***:* Create a 1 page new or updated, fresh, better than theirs resume. Use a Word resume template.

- **Project 2***: P*repare a 2 or 3 paragraph cover letter. Use a Word cover letter template.

Workshop 11   Project 1

A better than theirs job resume means that the resume helps to land a job interview. An updated resume usually will show social media presence. Look at the examples that show an unrevised and a revised, updated resume.

step 1: With Word open, look to the top of the screen on the Ribbon. Select File, New. A rectangular shape search for templates dialog box will appear. Key in the word resume.

step 2: Select a resume template of your choice. Download and save the template that you chose.

step 3: Follow the instructions on the template by typing your information over the place holder information.

step 4: Print 1 hard copy and place it in your class folder.

DARLA TOOTLE PARKER
12 Apple Court, Merryville, IL 60539

Phone: 631-123-7890	Email: jjmythe@yahoo.com

QUALIFICATIONS SUMMARY

Problem preventer skilled in domestic home management and shoestring budget management

Accomplishments: supervised a non-profit's successful 6-month car raffle fund raiser that quickly raised $75,000 to make much needed building repairs; managing to help send a child through college selling handmade items online

EXPERIENCE

June 1990 to present

Finance Secretary Volunteer

VFW Post 100, Merryville, IL

Provide guidance and support for new volunteers; find and implement new strategies/ideas for fund raising; keep books up-to-date

June 1989-1978

Part-time Tutor Volunteer

Parkview Baptist Church After School Program, Evansville, IL

After school developmental math tutor

August 1974-1978

President, PTA

Parkview High School, Evansville, IL

Listen, lead, plan, recruit, and teamwork to accomplish goals

EDUCATION

Certificate, Basic Computer Literacy, Carteret Senior Center, NC

Associate Degree, Secretarial Science, JFK Jr. College, Chicago, IL

SKILLS

Bookkeeping, basic computer skills—computer keyboarding, Word, PowerPoint, Quick Books

INTERESTS

Blogging; walking; designing & making 1-of-a-kind art greeting cards

DARLA TOOTLE PARKER

SKILLS

- computers: Microsoft Office Word and PowerPoint
- management: non-profit fund raising
- online business: 1-of-a-kind 3D artist greeting cards
- bookkeeping: Quick books software

OBJECTIVE

Part-time administrative support position

EXPERIENCE

Home Business Manager | Jaimee's Greeting Cards | 2010-Present

Building and updating websites, implementing marketing strategies, business social networking, developing "wow" effect new handmade cards

Accomplishment: managing to help send a child to college on a shoe string budget

Volunteer | VFW Post, PTA, and St. Luke After School Program | 1992-Present

2010-present VFW Post Finance secretary, bookkeeper, fund raiser, new volunteer trainer; 1997-2009 after school math tutor; 1992-1996 PTA goal accomplishing President

Accomplishment: Problem solving--helped to develop and supervise a non-profit car raffle fund raiser that within 6 months raised $75,000 to make much needed after Hurricane building repairs

EDUCATION

Computer Certificates | 2017-Present | Senior Center
Internet Skills, Microsoft Office Word, PowerPoint

Secretary Associate Degree | 1980 | JFK Jr. College
accounting, algebra, business communications, text editing, marketing, office management, business math

dtparker@yahoo.com
88 Beach Rd.
Wilmington, NC 28401

910-927-8418

www.linkedin.com/in/ darlaparker

http://twitter.com/ DarlasWorkPlaces

VOLUNTEER & LEADERSHIP EXPERIENCE

- secretary, developmental math tutor, high school PTA President
- supervisor: cash in a hurry non-profit fund raising volunteer: VFW finance

your better than theirs
resume hard copy

Workshop 11　Project 2

Prepare a better than theirs cover letter using a word processing template. A cover letter gives you a chance to enhance your resume by including something special or personal but interesting about relevant experience. A workshop participant who was finding a part-time job search a frustrating ordeal, was advised to start mentioning that he was the coach that helped lead his organization's baseball team to victory for the last 3 consecutive years. One of the largest employers in town, who had lost to their major competitor for many consecutive years, hired him even though they rarely hire anyone due to low turnover.

step 1: With Word open, look to the top of the screen on the Ribbon. Select File, New. A rectangular shape search for templates dialog box will appear. Key in the words cover letters.

step 2: Select a cover letter template of your choice. Download and save the template that you chose.

step 3: Follow the instructions on the template by typing your information over the place holder information.

step 4: Print 1 hard copy and place it in your class folder.

DARLA PARKER

DARLAP@YAHOO.COM

910-927-8418

88 Beach Rd.
Wilmington, NC 28401

MAJOR SMYTHE
HR DIRECTOR, LARGE MART, INC.
965 COMMERCE DR., AZ 87650

Dear Major Smythe, Director

The places where I work provide me with significant administrative support experience. I work as a finance secretary and online business manager. Associates indicate that I am a wiz with numbers and very good at team working to meet or exceed expectations like the time our agency raised $75,000 in less than six months. My technology skills are kept up-to-date by passing Senior Tech Academy courses. I was the program's valedictorian.

As requested at the Large Mart website, my resume is attached. To hire a part-time administrative support associate with a proven track record of support excellence, contact me.

Sincerely,

Darla Parker

your better than theirs
cover letter hard copy

Workshop 11   Self-Test

Short answer essay questions. Key a 1.5 multiple spaced response to each question using a sentence(s).

1. Do you think that the updated version of the Darla sample resume template—the one with the online resume links, would be more appealing to a potential employer that the original resume version?

2. Just how easy did you find using a resume template? Or, do you think it would have been easier for you to key your resume without using a template?

3. Can a document that you prepare be saved as a template? To help answer this question, you can look to the Ribbon and use the Help or Tell me what you want to do feature?

4. Is it necessary to have a resume and cover letter if you are applying for a job position online?

your Work Shop 11
self-test
short answer responses

WORKSHOP 12

Outsmart
Your Smart
Mobile Devices

Why did you mark my answer wrong?
Computers are smarter than people, right?

"Design is not what it looks and feels like. It's how it works." Steve Jobs

WORKSHOP 12   PROJECT 1

Want more out of your smart phone than you have been able to get on your own? This workshop will answer questions and guide you towards ways to become more proficient in the use of a smartphone. Take the smartphone survey.

SMARTPHONE SURVEY

_____Which <u>one</u> best describes how you feel about smartphones?
1. helpful
2. annoying
3. distracting
4. connecting
5. freedom
6. a leash

_____What <u>one</u> describes your thoughts this month about using a smartphone?

1. financial burden
2. worth the cost
3. couldn't live without it
4. not always needed
5. connecting
6. essential necessity

_____Do you have home Internet service--another way to get on the Internet at home other than a smartphone?

       1. Yes   2. No

_____What 5 things over the past month did you use a smartphone for the most? Select the top 5.

1. stream movies/videos/TV
2. music
3. text message
4. eMail
5. Internet use
6. directions
7. avoid boredom
8. social network
9. voice or video calling
10. local or national news
11. play games
12. take and send pictures
13. ignore others; avoid interaction
14. shop
15. pay for stuff
16. therapy
17. control home environment
18. baby sit
19. business
20. dating
21. start car

Ways To Outsmart Your Smartphone Activities

Activity 1: Purpose

way 1: Determine what you want to use a smartphone to do for you. This narrows down the list of how to outsmart. The best smartphone and tech gadgets of the year that cater to mature adult populations are at sites like this one: **www.tech50plus.com**. Are there any smartphone or related tech devices on this site that you currently have or would like to purchase?

Activity 2: Cost

way 2: Ascertain how much can or will pay. Goggle research the words cellphone smart rating. There are good seasonal and other promotional deals out there. Be sure to ask around among family and friends to see what they think about their smartphone vendor's prices and services.

Activity 3: Read and Keep—No Need to Weep

way 3: The stuff that comes in the smartphone box like warranty, accessories, written directions and onsite instructions—do not discard box and contents. It can be challenging to forego reading the instructions, but it is so very important to do this, first. Manufacturers have how-to web sites there for you to use. Use them. Many workshop participants find Youtube how-to videos one of the best sources of excellent, step by step instructtions that have them using a smartphone more quickly.

Activity 4: Tech Support
way 4: The apps—lifetime unlimited tech support. Use it—again, and again until you can master an app you would like to use more often!

Activity 5: Smart Phone Guru Tutor
way 5: Participant in a personal smartphone tutoring session. Get a tutor. Yes, a YouTube video or PowerPoint is alright, but a class speaker or personal tutor is often better. There are smartphone usage experts who will schedule a time to meet with you and show you how to use features of your smart phone. Some guru tutors are available online, too. Complete this activity for way 5—an optional activity.

Top 5 Features & How to Get Them to Work

On iPhone and Android devices, step by step instructions are provided by Adam Lui to show you how to configure your device to make it much easier and better to use when it comes to:
1. Enabling Zoom Magnification
2. Boosting the Size of Icons and Text
3. Enabling Spoken Audio Feedback
4. Making Text High-Contrast
5. Using Voice Commands (e.g. Siri for Apple Devices)

Need or want help using these features and more, go to this guru's website. Copy and paste this address in the URL box:

http://ctnbayarea.org/blog/5-ways-make-digital-devices-easier-seniors/. (Do not copy the punctuation period at the end of the address).

Workshop 12 Self-Test

1. What makes a smartphone so smart?

2. What are some devices or products now obsolete or becoming obsolete because of smart phones? Are dollars and cents plus checks becoming obsolete, too?

3. Are smartphones getting smarter?

4. Post a comment in the senior life blog for this workshop at:

   seniorlifetechblog.wordpress.com

Specify what you think is a problem or frustration of using smartphones. Identify something that you wish a smartphone would do for you—be creative or be practical. Can you imagine going for a walk in the park with a pet that is a walking, talking, computing, communicating new Dr. Canty Smart Phone Pet?

your workshop 12
self-test question responses

WORD PROCESSING COMPETENCY EXAM

Directions: Given 90 minutes, complete the word processing competency test without asking anyone to help you to complete it. **Double space** between tasks.

TASKS 1-5: Type and **center** these 5 items that consist of your:
Name
Address
City, State, Zip Code
email address
cell or telephone number

TASKS 6-7: Type your first name in **Verdana font** and **size 20**. **BOLD** and **UNDERLINE** your name. Select and **color** your name **a color of your choice**.

TASK 8: **Insert a picture** of any mobile device or computer. Yes, you can insert an appropriate image from the Internet.

TASKS 9-12: **Compose** a new **blog post comment** message at

seniorlifetechblog.wordpress.com

Post in Comments in the Contact section. The comment post should be about any topic of your choice related to technology. <u>Note</u>: Others may later be able to view comments.

TASKS 13-17: **Set LEFT** and **RIGHT Margins** for 1.5 inches. Evaluate this course and book by making a 3-item bullet list. Key and center the words **Word Processing Workshop Evaluation** as the title. The list should indicate:

- what you like about the workshop or book
- what could use improvement
- whether you would recommend the course to others

TASKS 18-20: **Save** the test document with a file name that contains your name and wptest like kenmccyberswptest.

- **Print** a hard copy.
- Send the completed exam to your professor as an **attachment** in an **email** message.

your competency exam
completed hard copy document

ABOUT THE AUTHOR

What Steve Jobs did with helping to place a computer in billions of pockets is somewhat similar to what Dr. Canty wants to do with computer technology basic literacy. Since 2004 to present, Dr. Canty is on a collaborative mission with community groups, colleges, universities, housing and senior centers plus website sites to help make communities with senior populations 100% computer literate. She wants to help spread computer technology literacy everywhere among adult populations that did not grow up using computers, starting with North Carolina—county by county, 1 byte at a time.

Senior Life Technology Classes/Workshops

Some of you might have participated in or read about senior life technology classes/workshops. The graduation celebrations are beautiful. Here is a synopsis from *The Wilmington Journal* articles.

The senior students dressed in the same color—white for women and black or navy for men. A wonderful speaker praised their efforts to the applause of a joyful audience filled with relatives and friends. The oldest graduate was 89. One highly dedicated student was selected as the valedictorian and received the prestigious Gates Mouse Pad Honor Award. A reception followed the awarding of certificates.

Dr. Canty, who since 2004 to present, collaborates with senior centers, colleges and community groups to spread senior citizen computer literacy everywhere, noticed that quite a few students were either retired military citizens, or spouses of retired military who had chosen to spend their "golden computer literate years" in the local region. The students enrolled in a morning or an afternoon class. The classes were offered at multiple campus locations, including a location in a low-income housing project's education center.

Each academy has a different celebration theme. One celebration was hosted to applaud the efforts of retired military veterans, spouses of military veterans, and civilian technology boot camp participants who are victoriously bridging the digital divide—one byte at a time.

SENIOR LIFE TECHNOLOGY WORKSHOPS
SOME PARTICIPANT AFFLIATIONS

Apostolic Community Church PAW, Inc.
Bowens Chapel AME Zion Church
Brunswick County Senior Resource Center
Cape Fear Baptist Church
Cape Fear Community College Continuing Ed.
Columbus County Senior Center, Ransom
Creekwood Housing Education Center
Disabled American Veterans (DAV)
Durham Center for Senior Life
East Columbus Senior Center
Ebenezer Missionary Baptist Church
First Baptist Missionary Church
First Born Holiness Church
Gregory Congregational Church
Johnson Chapel AMEZ Church
Hillcrest Housing Education Center
Leland Senior Center
Lighthouse Shining Ministries
Leon Mann Enrichment Center
Macedonia Fire Baptized Church
Macedonia Missionary Baptist Church
Moore's Chapel Missionary Baptist
Mt. Calvary Missionary Baptist Church
Mt. Nebo Baptist Church
Mt. Olive AME Church
Mt. Pilgrim Missionary Baptist Church
New Hanover County Senior Center
Prayer and Bible Church
Progressive Lodge #830
Shiloh Missionary Baptist Church
Shining Light Ministries
St. Andrews AME Zion Church
St. Luke AME Zion Church
St. Stephens AME Church
Summerville AMEZ Church
Union Missionary Baptist Church
United Senior Citizens Club
United States Air Force
United States Army
United States Civil Service
United States Marine Corps
United States Navy
University of North Carolina Wilmington OLLI
Veterans Foreign Wars (VFW)
Walter's Chapel AME Zion Church
Williston Alumni Class '62

New Senior Life
Computer Technology Workshops
Continuously Forming

New technology easy to read and to understand books and workshops are continuously under construction as technology changes. Interested in any of these workshops and under construction books? Let us know on your workshop class blog at https://seniorlife.tech.blog/.

1. **Coloring Book Construction—52 things To Do in Senior Life Tech Classes**

2. **I Am Going to Photoshop You—Scrape Book Page Making**

3. **I Have My Own Channel--See My New YouTube Video or Short Comic Strip**

4. **The New Grow & Prosper Mindset—Pass It On Project**

- *Robotics & The New You*
- *Yes, Seniors Can Code, Too*
- *Senior Life Technology: Newest Developments*
- *Want or Need PowerPoint Skills?*
- *Need or Want Desktop Publishing Skills?*

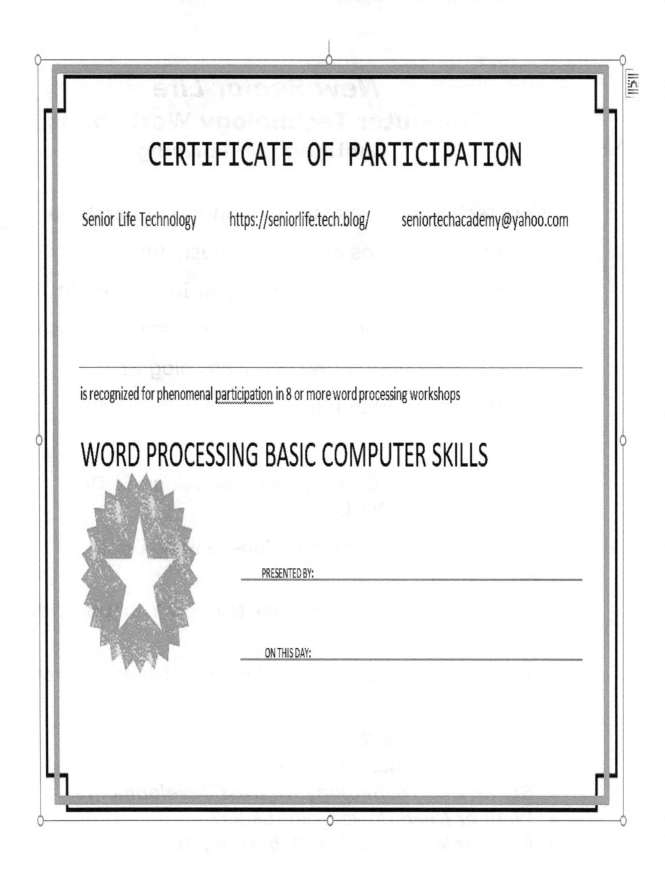

CERTIFICATE OF PARTICIPATION

Senior Life Technology   https://seniorlife.tech.blog/   seniortechacademy@yahoo.com

_____

is recognized for phenomenal participation in 8 or more word processing workshops

WORD PROCESSING BASIC COMPUTER SKILLS

PRESENTED BY: _____

ON THIS DAY: _____

Thanks for participating!

www.ingramcontent.com/pod-product-compliance
Lightning Source LLC
Chambersburg PA
CBHW060156060326
40690CB00018B/4132